LOW VOICE

# 28 AMERICAN ART SONGS

*for Low Voice and Piano*

ED 4600

ISBN 978-1-4950-0071-3

G. SCHIRMER, *Inc.*

DISTRIBUTED BY

Visit Hal Leonard Online at
**www.halleonard.com**

Contact us:
**Hal Leonard**
7777 West Bluemound Road
Milwaukee, WI 53213
Email: info@halleonard.com

In Europe, contact:
**Hal Leonard Europe Limited**
42 Wigmore Street
Marylebone, London, W1U 2RN
Email: info@halleonardeurope.com

In Australia, contact:
**Hal Leonard Australia Pty. Ltd.**
4 Lentara Court
Cheltenham, Victoria, 3192 Australia
Email: info@halleonard.com.au

# CONTENTS

# It's all I have to bring

Emily Dickinson*

Ernst Bacon

*Words printed by special permission.

wide. Be sure you count, should I for - get,— Some - one the sun could tell,—
richly
poco rit.
pp
This, and my heart, and all the bees
pp
Which in the clo - ver dwell.
rit.
rit.

# The Crucifixion
## from *Hermit Songs*

From The Speckled Book, 12th Century
Translated by Howard Mumford Jones

Samuel Barber
Op. 29, No. 5

Text from *Romanesque Lyric*, by permission of the University of North Carolina Press.

*f* *broadly*

Ah, sore was the suff-'ring borne By the bod-y of Ma-ry's

*f*

*con ped.*

*p* *tenderly and slower*

Son, But sor-er still to Him was the grief Which for His sake

*p*

*espr.*

(21) *mf* *p*

**Tempo I**

*allarg.*

Came up-on His Moth - er.

*allarg.*

*mf* *p* *mp* *p*

Oct. 26, 1952

*To Daisy*

# The Daisies

James Stephens

Samuel Barber
Op. 2, No. 1

Poem from *Collected Poems of James Stephens.* Printed by permission of The Macmillan Company, publishers.

The Windmill,
Rogers Park
July 20, 1927

*In Stephens' poem the word is "happily," which Barber chose to set on two notes rather than three.

# Hey nonny no!

**from *Three Songs: The Words from Old England***

Anonymous (16th century)

Samuel Barber

Is't not fine to swim in wine,
And turn up-on the toe,
faster
And sing hey non-ny no! When the winds blow and the seas flow?
slower
a tempo
Hey non-ny no!
Hey non-ny no! Hey non-ny no!
[cresc.]
[f]
faster
molto rit.
a tempo
Men are fools that wish to die!
8va

*To Isabelle Vengerova*

# The Monk and His Cat

**from *Hermit Songs***

8th or 9th century
Translated by W.H. Auden

Samuel Barber
Op. 29, No. 8

Words used by special permission.
*Notes marked (–) in these two measures should be slightly longer, pochissimo rubato; also on the fourth page. [Barber's footnote]

mf
p
For you it is hunt-ing, for me stud-y.
mf
p
Your shin - ing eye
simile
watch - es the wall;
p
my fee - ble eye is fixed on a
p
book.
f declamato
You re-joice when your claws En-trap a mouse;
8va
pp
f subito

p cantabile
rall.
I re-joice when my mind Fath-oms a prob-lem.
p
rall.
a tempo, tranquillo
mp
Pleased with his own art, Neith-er hin-ders the oth-er;
espr.
mp a tempo
mf
p
Thus we live e - ver With-out te-dium and en - vy.
mf
p
poco rall.
Tempo I
p
Pan-gur, white Pan - gur,
cantando la melodia
poco rall.
p

p
How hap - py we are A - lone to - geth-er, Scho-lar and
sempre in tempo
pp
cat.
Pan-gur, white Pan - gur,
mf
pp
p espr.
How hap - py we are.
ten.
senza rall.
pp
senza ped.
(in tempo)
pp

Feb. 16, 1953

# A Slumber Song of the Madonna

Alfred Noyes

Samuel Barber

**Moderato**

*p* *peacefully, but never lightly*

Sleep, lit - tle ba - by, I love thee;

Sleep, lit - tle king, I am bend - ing a - bove thee;

How should I know what to sing?

*p* *peacefully, but never lightly*

*f*

*f*

p
Here in my arms as I sing thee to sleep! Hush - a - by
p

Poco più mosso
mf
low, Rock - a - by so. Kings may have won - der - ful
mf

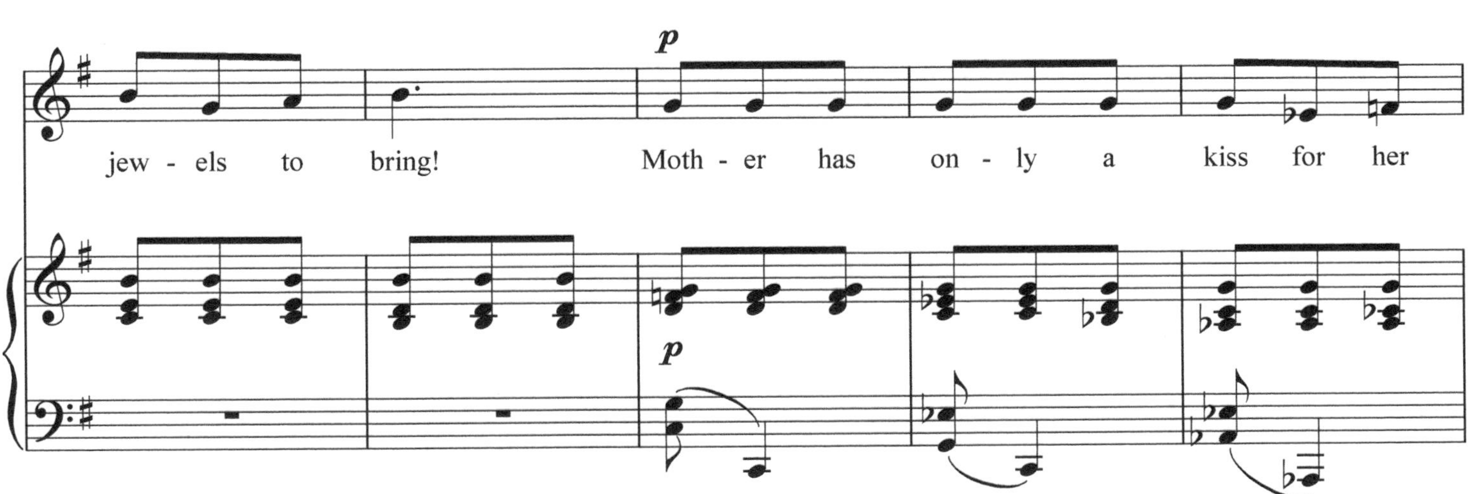
p
jew - els to bring! Moth - er has on - ly a kiss for her
p

cresc. poco a poco
ff
king. Why should my sing - ing So make me to weep?
cresc. poco a poco
ff [ rit. ]
pp fervently
On - ly I know that I love thee, I love thee!
[ quasi a tempo, ma poco lento ]
sub. pp
[ rit. ]
Tempo primo
pp
Love thee, my lit - tle one, Sleep!
p
pp

# Mother, I cannot mind my wheel

Walter Savage Landor

Samuel Barber

O, if you felt the pain I feel! But
O, who ev - er felt as I?
No long - er
could I doubt him true—
All oth - er

men may use de - ceit;
[cresc.]
[mf]
[dim.] [poco rit.]
He al - ways said my eyes were
[mf]
[dim.] [poco rit.]
blue, And of - ten swore my lips were
[a tempo]
[p]
[poco rit.]
sweet.
[a tempo]
[p]
[poco rit.]

*To Sara*

# Sure on this shining night

James Agee

Samuel Barber
Op. 13, No. 3

Text from *Permit Me Voyage*. Used by permission of Yale University Press, Publishers.

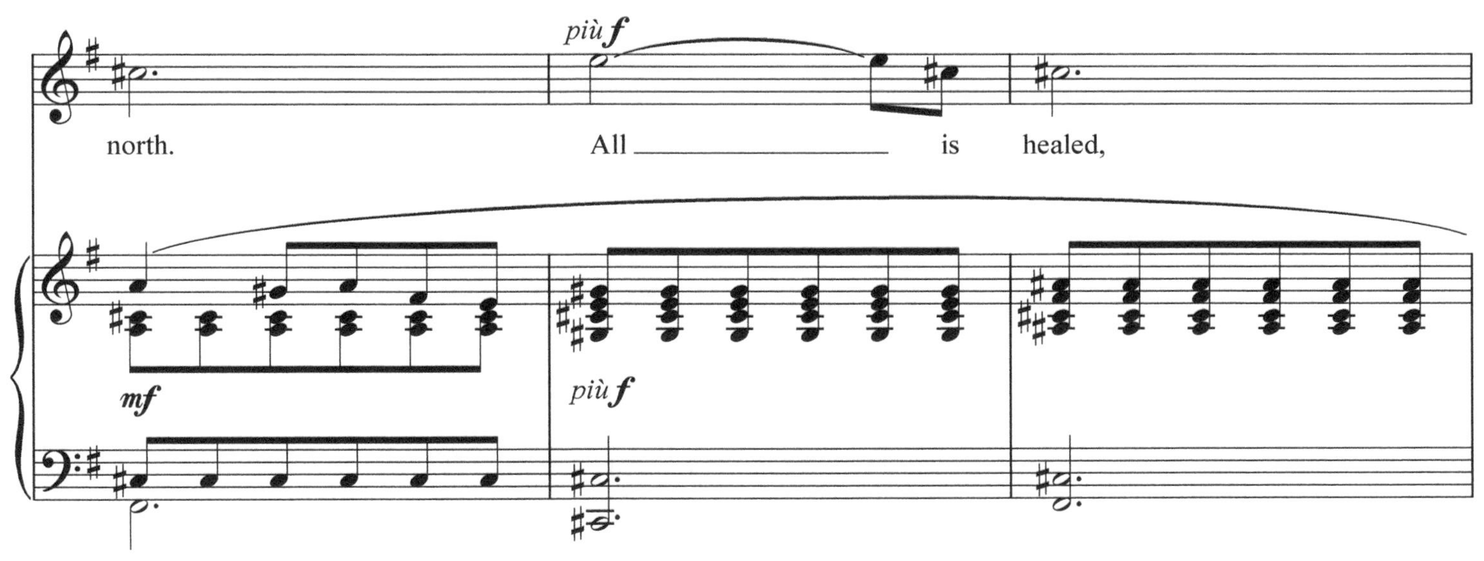
più f
north.
All
is
healed,
mf
più f

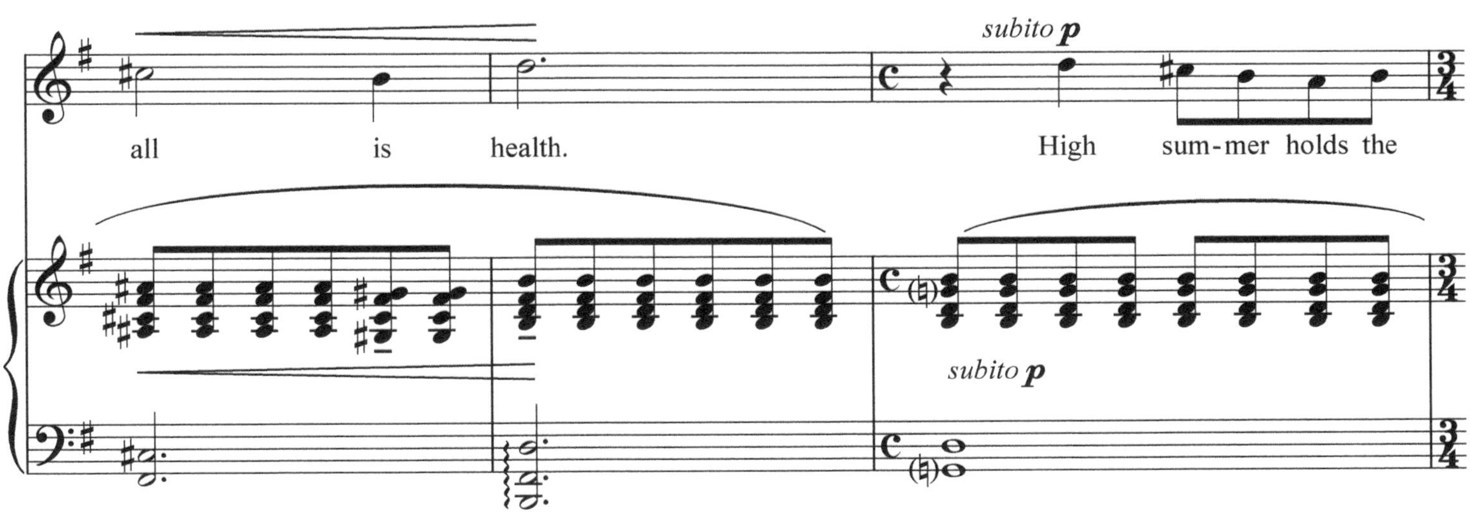
subito p
all
is
health.
High
sum-mer holds the
subito p

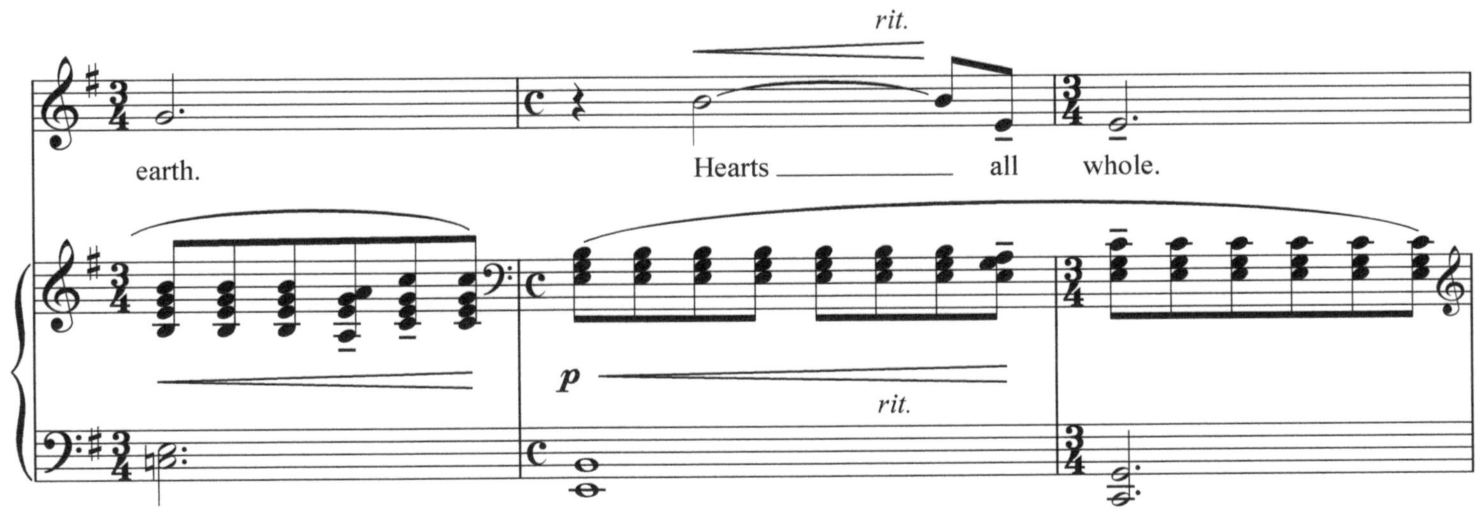
rit.
earth.
Hearts
all
whole.
p
rit.

September 1938

# Heavenly Grass

Tennessee Williams

Paul Bowles

♩ = 52
feet took a walk In heav - en-ly grass. All night while the lone - some
♩ = 66
stars rolled past, Then my feet come down to walk on earth And my
f
molto rit.
♩ = 52
moth - er cried When she give me birth.
pp
molto rit.
p
p

♩ = 66
Now my feet walk _ far And my
mf
♩ = 52
p
pp poco
feet _ walk_ fast, But they still got an itch for _ heav - en-ly grass. But they
p
pp poco
meno mosso
still got an itch for _ heav'n - ly grass. _
meno mosso
molto rit.
8
ppp

# Cabin

Tennessee Williams

Paul Bowles

mosso
lift - ed the latch for a man or a storm. Now the
cab - in falls to the win - ter wind and the walls cave in where they
kissed and sinned. And the long white rain sweeps
clean the room like a white - haired witch with a long straw broom!
molto rit.
Tempo I°
meno mosso
molto ritardando

# Sugar in the Cane

Tennessee Williams

Paul Bowles

3
ba - ker.
I'm sweet sug - ar in the cane,
Nev - er touched ex - cept by rain.
If you touched me God save you, These sum - mer days are hot and blue.

p
segue
8vb
loco
mf
I'm po - ta - toes not yet mashed,
segue
mf
I'm a check that ain't been
cashed.
I'm a win - dow with a blind,

Can't see what goes on be - hind.
If you did, God save your soul! These win - ter nights are blue and
cold!
ten.
8vb

*To Sophie Sargent*

# The Lamb

William Blake

Theodore Chanler

rit.
Gave thee such a ten - der voice,
Mak - ing all the vales re - joice?
p dolce
rit.
a tempo, semplice
rit.
Lit - tle Lamb, who made thee?
Dost thou know who made thee?
a tempo
semplice
rit.
Ped.
Ped.
a tempo
a tempo
poco rit.
p a tempo
Lit - tle Lamb, I'll tell thee,
Lit - tle Lamb, I'll tell thee:
a tempo
Ped.
Ped.

He is call - èd by thy name, For He calls Him - self a Lamb.
poco cresc.
He is meek, and He is mild; He be - came a lit - tle child.
dim.
rit.
I a child, and thou a lamb, We are call - èd by His name.
p dolce
rit.
a tempo, semplice
rit.
Lit - tle Lamb, God bless thee! Lit - tle Lamb, God bless thee!
a tempo
semplice
rit.

*To P. G.*

# When I Have Sung My Songs

Words and Music by
Ernest Charles

agitato
Just you and I.
I could not share them all a -
accel. - al - agitato
mf
cresc.
gain–
I'd rath - er
die
With just the
cresc. sempre
thought
that I had loved
so well,
so
f
meno f
ff
meno f

agitato
true, That I could nev - er sing a - gain,
mf
f
ff
That I could nev - er, nev - er sing a - gain, Ex - cept to
mf
ff
dim.
you.
ten.
mf
rit.
p

*To Lawrence Tibbett*

# Loveliest of Trees

A. E. Housman*

John Duke

*Poem from "A Shropshire Lad." Printed by permission of Grant Richards, London, publisher.

now Is hung with bloom a - long the
cresc.
dim.
bough, And stands a - bout the wood - land
mf
ride Wear - ing white for East - er - tide.
p

cresc.
poco f
f più animato
Now, of my three - score years and ten.
più animato
mf
Twen - ty will not come a - gain,

mf
3
cresc.
And take from sev - en - ty springs a
score, It on - - ly leaves me
f
p
Ped.
fif - - ty more.
poco f
pp subito
Ped.

pp
And since to look at things in bloom
tranquillo e sempre pp
Ped.
Fif - ty springs are lit - tle room,
pp
A - bout the wood - lands I will go To
pp
mp

poco rit.
see the cher - ry hung with
poco rit.
a tempo
snow.
a tempo
pp
mp
pp

*To George Hamlin*

# Do not go, my love

Words by
Sir Rabindranath Tagore

Music by
Richard Hageman

lose you when I am sleep - - ing.
Ped. *
Do not go, my love,
Ped. *
f
with-out ask-ing my leave.
mf
f
Più mosso
I start up and stretch my
ff
pp subito
sostenuto
dolce

hands to touch you.
rall.
I ask my-self, "Is it a dream?"
pp
pp
a tempo
ppp
due ped.
Could I but en-tan-gle your feet with my

heart, and hold them fast to my
breast!
Adagio
Do not
rall. molto
pp
go, my love, with-out ask ing my leave.
m. s.
rall.
pp

*to the Guide*

# Where the Music Comes From

Words and Music by
Lee Hoiby

how. I want to sing to the ear-ly morn - ing, See the
sun - light melt the snow; And oh, I want to
grow.
I want to
f
p

wake to the liv - ing spir - it Here in - side me where it lies. I want to
mf
p
lis - ten till I can hear it, Let it guide me, and re - al - ize That I can
go with the flow un - end - ing, That is blend - ing, that is
real; And oh, I want to
f

feel.
p
I want to
walk in the earth - ly gar - den, Far from cit - ies, far from
mf
fear. I want to talk to the grow - ing gar - den, To the

*pronounced *day – vas* (nature spirits)

# Serenity

John Greenleaf Whittier
(from *The Brewing of Soma*)

Charles Ives
(adapted 1919)

# In the mornin'

Negro spiritual (before 1850) communicated to Ives in 1929 by Mary Evelyn Stiles

Accompaniment by Charles Ives

slower
Slowly
Give me Je - sus!
'Twixt the cra - dle and the grave,
'Twixt the cra - dle and the grave,
'Twixt the cra - dle and the grave,
Chorus
più animato
Give me Je - sus!
Give me Je - sus, Give me Je - sus;
rit.
poco ten.
You can have all the world, but Give me Je - sus!

*To Mme. Povla Frijsh*

# The Pasture

Robert Frost*

Charles Naginski

*From "Collected Poems" by Robert Frost. By permission of Henry Holt and Company, Publishers.

wait to watch the wa - ter clear, I may):

I sha'n't be gone long.– You come too.
mf

I'm go-ing out to fetch the lit - tle calf That's stand-ing by the
p

moth - er.
It's so young, It totters when she
licks it with her tongue.
mf
poco rall.
I sha'n't be gone long.— You come too.
8
p
poco rall.

*To Miriam Witkin*



# The Green Dog

Words and Music by
Herbert Kingsley

mp
on it.
Shoes of leaf - green,
Hose of tea - green, Coat of ap - ple - green, Gloves of bot - tle - green,
In fact, I nev - er would be seen
ex - cept in
8va
mf
rit.
a tempo
green
If my dog were green.
rit.
f a tempo

But, a - las! no mat - ter what you've heard, The facts are con - sis - tent - ly ab -
surd,
For my dog is - n't green,
l.h.
l.h.
l.h.
And, what sets the mat - ter e - ven more a - gog—
ff
I have - n't an - y dog!
mf
colla voce
fff

# Black is the color of my true love's hair

Text collected and adapted by
John Jacob Niles
Music by John Jacob Niles

love — the grass where - on she stands.
mf
I — love my — love and — well she knows, I
love — the grass where - on she goes; If — she on — earth no —
mf
p

*Troublesome Creek, which empties into the Kentucky River.

mf
Black, black, black is the col - or of my
mf
true love's hair, Her lips are some-thing ro - sy fair, The
pert - est face and the dain-ti - est hands— I love the grass where-
on she stands.
mf
dim.
p
pp

# Go 'way from my window

Words and Music by
John Jacob Niles
Arranged by the composer

both-er me no more. I'll
long as song-birds sing. I'll
on ac-count of you. Go
real-ly did love best. Go 'way from my win-dow, Go
'way from my door, Go 'way, 'way, 'way from my bed-side And
mf
3
rit. e dim.
both-er me no more, And both-er me no more.

# The Lass from the Low Countree

Text adapted by J.J.N.

Music by
John Jacob Niles

mp
sor - row! Now she sleeps in the val - ley where the wild - flow - ers nod, And
mp
dim.
no one knows she loved him but her - self and God.
p
One
dim.
p
mf
morn, when the sun was on the mead, He passed by her door on a
mf

milk-white steed;_ She smil-ed and she spoke, but he paid no heed. Oh,
sor - row, sing sor - row! Now she sleeps in the val - ley where the
wild - flow-ers nod, And no one knows she loved him but her - self and God.
If you be a lass from the Low Coun-tree, Don't
p
mp
dim.

mf
love of no lord of high de gree; They hain't got a heart for
sym - pa - thy. Oh, sor - row, sing sor - row! Now she
sleeps in the val - ley where the wild - flow - ers nod, And
dim.
no one knows she loved him but her - self and God.
mf
f
p
mp
dim.
pp

*To Helen-Claire Moyle*

# American Lullaby

Words and Music by
Gladys Rich

keep-ing the wolf from the door.
mf
mf
Nurs-ie will raise the win-dow shade high,
So you can see the
mf
cars whiz-zing by.
poco accel.
f
mp a tempo
Home in a hur - ry each Dad-dy must fly To a
a tempo
poco accel.
f

mp
ba - by like you.
mf
Hush - a - bye, you sweet lit - tle ba - by, And
p
close those pret - ty blue eyes.
Moth - er has gone to her
week - ly bridge par - ty To get her wee ba - by the prize.
3

mf
Nurs-ie will turn the ra-di-o on,
mf
So you can hear a sleep-y-time song,
rall.
mf
mp
a tempo
Sung by a la-dy whose poor heart must long For a
rall.
a tempo
mf
ba-by like you!
3
dim. e rall.

*For Giuseppe De Luca*

# This Little Rose

Emily Dickinson*

William Roy

*Poem copyright © 1945, by Millicent Todd Bingham.

thee.
slightly accelerated
mp
p
On-ly a bee will miss it,
On-ly a but - ter - fly,
p
Hast-en-ing from far jour - ney
On its breast to lie.
slightly accelerated
mp cresc.
slightly ac -
mf

mf
3
celerated
On-ly a bird will won-der,
a tempo
mf
3
3
sensitively
mp
On-ly a breeze will sigh,
Ah, lit-tle rose, how eas - y
mp
3
rit.
p a tempo
For such as thee to die!
a tempo
slightly accelerated
rit.
p
p
mp

# Holiday Song

Genevieve Taggard*

William Schuman
Arranged by the composer

*Words printed by exclusive permission.
**LH 8vb octaves in original key from ** to †

rit.
Fast, with great animation
mp
ff subito
Mm
Lo!
rit.
ff
simile sempre
Dee-de-lee dee, dee-de-lee dee, Lo! Dee-de-lee dee,
simile sempre
dee-de-lee dee, Lo! Dee-de-lee dee, dee-de-lee dee,
mf
mf
mp
Dee - de - lee, dee - de - lee, Lo!

**LH 8vb in original key from ** to †

all of us, ev - 'ry - one of us, ev - 'ry - one of us, ev - 'ry - one of us,
ev - 'ry - one of us, all of us, ev - 'ry - one, all of us,
𝅗𝅥 = 𝅗𝅥. preceding
fff
ev - 'ry - one, all of us, ev - 'ry - one of us has
fff
𝅗𝅥 = 𝅗𝅥
some - thing to sing a - bout, has some - thing to sing a -
8vb

New Rochelle, N.Y.
May 26, 1942
Arranged for solo voice May, 1946

**LH 8vb in original key from ** to †

# Orpheus with his lute

William Shakespeare
(From "Henry VIII")

William Schuman

mf
show'rs There had made a last - ing spring.
Ev - 'ry thing that heard him
Ped.
*
mp
play,
E-ven the bil-lows of the sea,
Hung their heads, and then lay
3
Ped.
*
p
by.
In sweet mu - sic is such art,
Kill-ing care and grief of
heart,
Fall a - sleep,
or hear - ing,
die.

# Brother Will, Brother John

Elizabeth Charles Welborn

John Sacco

ain't no use, Mis - ter, af - ter you're gone, — You
can't take it with you, Broth - er Will, Broth - er John.
You need - n't squeeze your coin tight in your hand, No
r.h.
place for small change in the Prom - ised Land. It

ain't no use, Mis - ter, af - ter you're gone, You
can't take it with you, Broth - er Will, Broth - er John.
sly, provocative
Shake a leg here, shake a leg there,
laugh a lit - tle, smile a lit - tle, spread a lit - tle cheer, Broth - er

Will, Broth - er John, Broth - er Will, Broth - er John, Broth - er
r.h.
Will, Broth-er John.
f freely
Why mope a - round with fu - ne - re - al fac - es, Whip up your nag and
sfz colla voce
loos - en the trac - es.
a tempo, slyly
Take a lit - tle joy, take a lit - tle plea - sure,
a tempo

Bow to the la - dies, dance a mea - sure, Broth - er
Will, Broth - er John, Broth - er Will, Broth - er John, Broth - er
r.h.
Will, Broth - er John.
f
You'll have to leave it when the cof - fin lid's on, You
f

mp
can't take it with you, Broth - er Will, Broth - er John, Broth - er
mp
cresc.
Will, Broth - er John, Broth - er Will, Broth - er John, Broth - er
f
Will, Broth - er John!
8va
f
8va
gliss.
sfz
sfz